‘The members of the Ch… ist of Latter-Day Saints … the biblical go… e Gospel wit… angelical Chri… hat has sent m…

Dr. E… , Pastor of Education and Evangelism at The First Baptist Church of Provo, Utah; itinerant preacher; evangelist.

‘A really helpful guide that will not only help you better understand what Mormons believe but will practically equip you to share the good news with them. Buy it. Read it. Put it into practice!’

Michael Ots, evangelist and author

‘I have been privileged to work in ministry with Tony in recent years. He has a great love for the Lord and is gifted with a remarkable faculty for explanation. He is also a seasoned evangelist and brings to this book his own experience in witnessing to Mormons. As a former Mormon apologist, I wholeheartedly recommend it to anyone wishing to better understand and witness to Mormons.’

Michael Thomas, Chairman, Reachout Trust

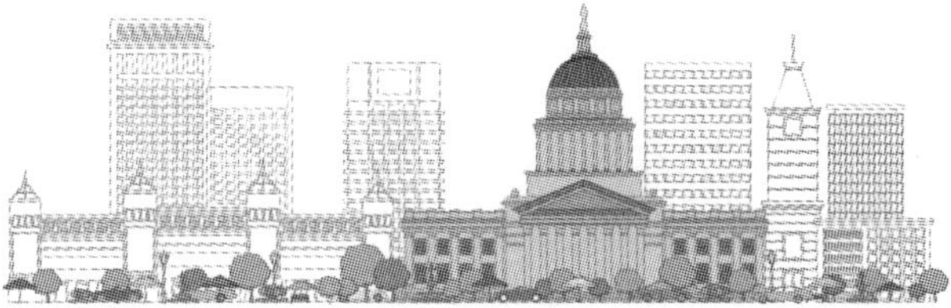

SHARING THE GOSPEL

WITH A MORMON

Also in this series:

Sharing the Gospel with a Jehovah's Witness
by Tony Brown

Sharing the Gospel with a Muslim Neighbour
by Robert Scott

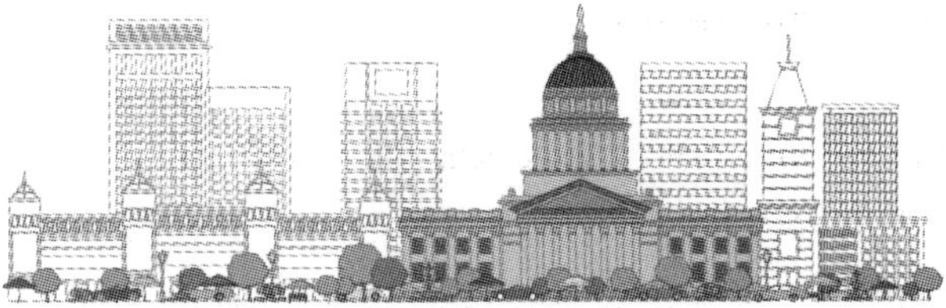

SHARING THE GOSPEL

WITH A

MORMON

TONY BROWN

10 Publishing

First published in Great Britain in 2023

British Library Cataloguing in Publication Data
A record for this book is available from the British Library

ISBN: 978-1-914966-20-0

Designed and typeset by Pete Barnsley (CreativeHoot.com)

Printed in Denmark

10Publishing, a division of 10ofthose.com
Unit C, Tomlinson Road, Leyland, PR25 2DY, England

Email: info@10ofthose.com
Website: www.10ofthose.com

1 3 5 7 10 8 6 4 2

For Cath, my wife, and our children, Josh, Beth and Joel. May they continue in the grace of God and the freedom found only in Jesus.

CONTENTS

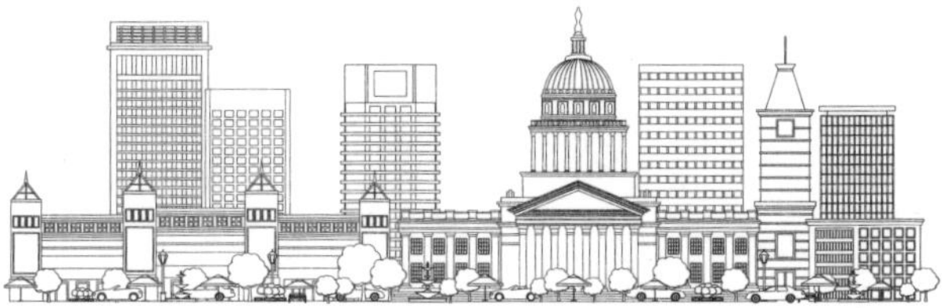

INTRODUCTION:

SPEAKING THE TRUTH IN LOVE

I love Mormons. I find myself strangely drawn to them. They are some of the kindest, hardest-working, most helpful and honourable people you could ever meet. They value what I value. They are moral and upright, love their families and have a real desire to serve God. Your question following my declared love for them may be: So, why are you not a Mormon?

The answer is this: Though I love Mormons, I do not love Mormonism.

IT'S NOT CHRISTIANITY

Mormonism is much like the military. It can take a person and smarten them up. By following its dictates, a person can discover a sense of purpose, live by a moral code, feel valuable and find themselves part of a bigger, close-knit community. But there is something Mormonism cannot do – it cannot save.

In this brief look at what Mormonism teaches, we will see that it is as far from orthodox, historic, biblical Christianity as it could possibly be. Therefore, as lovely as they can be, Mormons are a lost people who need to hear, and respond to, the real gospel. As we seek to communicate the way of salvation with them, we need to *speak the truth in love*. By doing so, we can show them that we are not anti-Mormon (a term they use against any who challenge them), but are anti-Mormonism.

My prayer is that this book will not only give you information and tools to use as you speak to them, but will also generate within you a love for the people we call Mormons.

1

THE PEOPLE FORMERLY KNOWN AS MORMONS

... for I contend that the Latter-day Saints are the only good and true Christians, that I know anything about in the world. There are a good many people who profess to be Christians, but they are not founded on the foundation that Jesus Christ himself has laid (Joseph Fielding Smith).[1]

MORMON MISSIONARIES

You can usually spot Mormons who knock at your door. They will be two smartly dressed young men, wearing suits, white shirts and ties. With their clean-cut images and a tidy haircut, they will also often, though not exclusively, have American accents. If you are still unsure who they are, check their name badges. Though typically aged between eighteen and twenty-five, they are inexplicably called 'Elder'. This badge identifies them as missionaries for The Church of Jesus Christ of Latter-day Saints.

TIP:

Though more commonly known by the nickname 'Mormons', which has stuck since the 1800s, they refer to themselves as Latter-day Saints, or 'LDS' for short. In 2018 President Russell M. Nelson announced that God had told him the Church should drop the moniker 'Mormons'.

Despite LDS missionaries usually being young men, they can also be female – 'Sisters' (who the

Mormon leadership has decided will typically be aged between nineteen and twenty-five) – or an older retired couple.

To 'serve a mission' for the Church of Jesus Christ of Latter-day Saints is like a rite of passage for young Mormons. Parents hope that their children will heed the call and make them proud, proving themselves faithful to the only true and living Church of Jesus Christ on the earth today. Though spoken of as a choice, there is a certain amount of pressure applied to help you make the 'right' decision:

> *We affirm that missionary work is a priesthood duty – and we encourage all young men who are worthy and who are physically able and mentally capable to respond to the call to serve. Many young women also serve, but they are not under the same mandate to serve as are the young men. We assure the young sisters of the Church, however, that they make a valuable contribution as missionaries, and we welcome their service (Thomas S. Monson).*[2]

THE MISSION SHOULD YOU CHOOSE TO ACCEPT IT

The 'mission' to which these young people hope to be called will be costly. It will require men to spend two years separated from their families, and women to spend eighteen months away from home. The funding for the mission must be raised by these young people themselves. There are also certain requirements of 'personal worthiness' that must be met, meaning that not every young LDS member can serve a mission even if they would like to do so. Those who go on mission must:

- Have faith in and a testimony of Heavenly Father; His Son, Jesus Christ; and the Holy Ghost
- Have a testimony of the Atonement of Jesus Christ and His role as the Saviour
- Have a testimony of the Prophet Joseph Smith and the restoration of the gospel
- Sustain the church authorities
- Keep the law of chastity (including avoiding pornography in any form)

- Keep the covenants made at baptism and elsewhere
- Attend all their church meetings
- Be honest in their dealings with others
- Pay a full tithing
- Keep the Word of Wisdom (a health code which, amongst other things, forbids them to drink tea and coffee)

TIP:

The Mormon name for God the Father is 'Heavenly Father'.

If young people pass this 'worthiness' test, they then eagerly await the letter of confirmation to drop through their letterbox. This will tell them where in the world they will serve as a missionary for the Church of Jesus Christ of Latter-day Saints.

MISSION IMPOSSIBLE

Wherever a young missionary is sent in the world, their first stopping-off point will be a Missionary Training Centre (MTC). Would-be missionaries spend around three weeks there, but longer if they need to learn a new language.

The key learning manual whilst at an MTC is called *Preach My Gospel*. This document begins by saying that the aim of a missionary is to: 'Invite others to come unto Christ by helping them receive the restored gospel through faith in Jesus Christ and His Atonement, repentance, baptism, receiving the gift of the Holy Ghost, and enduring to the end.'

Notice here words peculiar to Mormonism: they believe theirs is a 'restored' gospel. They teach that after the death of the apostles, the church became apostate and, hence, lost its authority. God 'restored' this authority to the church through the Prophet Joseph Smith. Therefore, they maintain the Church of Jesus Christ of Latter-day Saints alone has God's blessing and authority.

One implication of this is that if you are a baptised Christian who converts to Mormonism (I urge you not to do that), your previous baptism will be seen as invalid. You will need to be baptised by someone who has the proper 'priesthood authority'. Their Articles of Faith describes baptism as the first saving ordinance of the gospel (Article 1:4). It is through baptism and confirmation by priesthood authority that someone becomes a member of The Church of Jesus Christ of Latter-day Saints.

PRIESTHOOD AUTHORITY?

Mormon doctrine teaches that this priesthood is the power and authority of God given to man. A priesthood holder in the church has the authority both to perform ordinances and to act as a church leader.

Mormon history teaches that the Aaronic priesthood was given to Joseph Smith and Oliver Cowdery by John the Baptist. Shortly thereafter, the Melchizedek priesthood was conferred upon Joseph Smith by the apostles Peter, James and John. These two priesthoods were then passed down through Joseph Smith to other males within the group. Currently, qualified males aged twelve or older can receive the Aaronic priesthood, and qualified males who are eighteen or older can receive the Melchizedek priesthood.

However, the Bible tells us that Jesus is our priest:

Since then we have a great high priest who has passed through the heavens, Jesus, the Son of God, let us hold fast our confession. For we do not have a high priest who is unable to sympathize with our weaknesses, but one who in every respect has been tempted as we are, yet without sin. Let us then with confidence draw near to the throne of grace, that we may receive mercy and find grace to help in time of need (Hebrews 4:14–16).

TIP:

The book of Hebrews says that we need only one Priest – the Lord Jesus Christ.

PREACH MY GOSPEL

The *Preach My Gospel* manual is an evangelistic tool used by the missionaries. Their hope is that people will agree to five study sessions with them in which they will cover the following themes:

1. The message of the restoration of the gospel of Jesus Christ
2. The plan of salvation

3. The gospel of Jesus Christ
4. The commandments
5. Laws and ordinances

The topics build upon each other, with the missionaries seeking to convince people that the Church of Jesus Christ is the one true church. Throughout their presentations, Mormon missionaries will encourage the potential convert to do the following:

- Read the Book of Mormon
- Pray about the Book of Mormon
- Be baptised into the Mormon Church

THE BOOK OF MORMON

It will not take the missionaries long to introduce you to the Book of Mormon. They will be especially keen to show you, and have you read, Moroni 10:3–5:

> *Behold, I would exhort you that when ye shall read these things, if it be wisdom in God that ye should read them, that ye would remember*

> *how merciful the Lord hath been unto the children of men, from the creation of Adam even down until the time that ye shall receive these things, and ponder it in your hearts.*
>
> *And when ye shall receive these things, I would exhort you that ye would ask God, the Eternal Father, in the name of Christ, if these things are not true; and if ye shall ask with a sincere heart, with real intent, having faith in Christ, he will manifest the truth of it unto you, by the power of the Holy Ghost.*
>
> *And by the power of the Holy Ghost ye may know the truth of all things.*

Having read this, they will ask you to pray to God about the Book of Mormon. They believe that if you do so 'with a sincere heart, with real intent, having faith in Christ', God will give you an answer. You will receive confirmation of its authenticity as the Word of God via a 'burning in the bosom' – a feeling that the Mormon Church teaches can be used for determining all truth.

'I HAVE A FEELING'

Many of us have experienced a 'burning in the bosom', but it usually subsides after a couple of spoons of Gaviscon (or other heartburn remedies). This shows that a feeling, though it may accompany truth, is not by itself an infallible guide. Feelings can come from eating a dodgy chicken curry, from our own imaginings or from the enemy of truth – Satan. Feelings, contrary to what The Church of Jesus Christ of Latter-day Saints states, cannot authenticate truth. John Piper, a renowned Bible theologian, puts it like this:

> *My feelings are not God. God is God. My feelings do not define truth. God's word defines truth. My feelings are echoes and responses to what my mind perceives. And sometimes – many times – my feelings are out of sync with the truth. When that happens – and it happens every day in some measure – I try not to bend the truth to justify my imperfect feelings, but rather, I plead with God: Purify my perceptions of your truth and transform my feelings so that they are in sync with the truth.*[3]

Feelings come from the seat of our emotions – the heart – but the Bible is clear that the heart is not something we trust:

> *The heart is deceitful above all things, and desperately sick; who can understand it? (Jeremiah 17:9).*

So, if we cannot test whether something is true by feelings, how should this be done? The book of Acts gives us a good example:

> *Now these Jews were more noble than those in Thessalonica; they received the word with all eagerness, examining the Scriptures daily to see if these things were so (Acts 17:11).*

Here we find the Berean Jews being commended because they examined 'the Scriptures daily' to test if what they were being told by Paul and Silas was true. We need to do the same.

QUESTIONS FOR MORMON MISSIONARIES

As a way of illustrating this to missionaries, I have used the following imaginary scenario. If this isn't applicable to you, create a different scenario.

Me: I have started to have feelings for a young woman I work with. Should I trust my feelings and trade my wife in for a younger model?

Missionaries: No, that would be wrong.

Me: But I have such a strong feeling that this is 'true' love. You might even say that I feel a 'burning in my bosom'.

Missionaries: No, that would be wrong.

Me: Why is it wrong? Can't this feeling be the Holy Ghost?

Missionaries: No, that cannot be the Holy Ghost.

Me: How do you know? How can I know whether this feeling that I should leave my wife is from God or not?

CONTINUE ↓

> The purpose here is to get the missionaries to say that my feeling of leaving my wife for another woman is wrong because the Bible says it's wrong! My feelings, however strong they appear, are not what determines truth. God's Word determines truth!

The Protestant Reformer Martin Luther put it well:

Feelings come and feelings go,
And feelings are deceiving;
My warrant is the Word of God –
Naught else is worth believing.

Though all my heart should feel condemned
For want of some sweet token,
There is One greater than my heart
Whose Word cannot be broken.

I'll trust in God's unchanging Word
Till soul and body sever,
For, though all things shall pass away,
HIS WORD SHALL STAND FOREVER!

Sadly, the internal feeling that Mormons often describe as a 'burning' persuades them that the Book of Mormon is another testament of Jesus Christ. This then acts like a gateway drug which leads them onto something far more addictive and harmful. Once they have received 'testimony' from the Holy Ghost that the Book of Mormon is true, they then buy into Mormonism itself. But note this: the Book of Mormon contains little, to nothing, of what the new convert will go on to believe and teach.

TIP:

Get the missionaries' mobile number. LDS missionaries are moved around during their mission, but that mobile number will stay with the new incoming missionaries. Therefore, once you have that mobile number, you will have an ongoing opportunity to share the gospel with the new, and future, missionaries. If they have recorded your name and number, you may even find that the new missionaries will contact you.

2

'WE ARE CHRISTIANS'

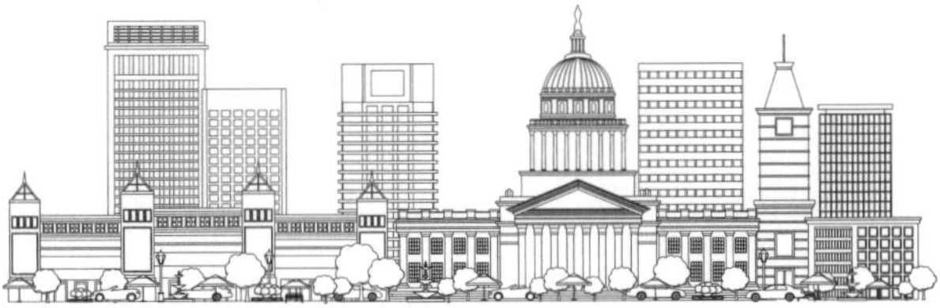

Are we Christians? Of course we are! No one can honestly deny that.

We may be somewhat different from the traditional pattern of Christianity. But no one believes more literally in the redemption wrought by the Lord Jesus Christ.

No one believes more fundamentally that He was the Son of God, that He died for the sins of mankind, that He rose from the grave, and that He is the living resurrected Son of the living Father (Gordon B. Hinckley).[4]

A CHRISTIAN APPEARANCE

Have you ever seen or heard the Osmonds? (If you are too young to have done so, use Google!) Clean-cut, teetotal and painfully polite, this family musical group, who are all Mormons, seem the embodiment of what it means to be a follower of the Lord Jesus Christ.

Mormons are adamant that they are Christians, and they will strenuously defend their right to be called such. I have not had many Mormon missionaries get angry with me but on one occasion, when I dared to suggest that they are not Christians, I experienced a Mormon meltdown.

The frustrated missionary took his name badge from his lapel and slammed it down on the table in front of me. He said, 'What does this say? It says we are the Church of JESUS CHRIST of Latter-day Saints.' I then apologised, but of course I still could not say that I believed he was a Christian.

If merely using the name Jesus Christ, or in this case having his name engraved on our badge, means you are a Christian, then I guess whenever my Muslim friend Abu says he believes in Jesus, he must be a Christian also.

DUBIOUS DOUBLESPEAK

On the surface, Mormonism certainly appears Christian. In dialogue with members of the Church of Jesus Christ of Latter-day Saints, you will find a commonality of language. They will speak in a Christian way, but beware: the words they use are interpreted in a Mormon way.

For example, a Mormon may say, 'We believe that Jesus Christ is the Son of God and the Saviour of the world. By His death and resurrection, we can be forgiven of our sin and return to heaven when we die.'

You may be tempted to respond by saying, 'Wow, you are a Christian.' But if this is you, then just hold those horses! Though what they say sounds thoroughly Christian, their interpretation of many of those words will be vastly different from biblical Christianity.

Consider this. Rather than asking the question 'Are Mormons Christian?', we may perhaps ask a different question: 'Is the Church of Jesus Christ of Latter-day Saints a Christian Church?' This puts the emphasis upon LDS doctrine rather than calling into question the beliefs and practices of individual Mormons, which can vary widely.

If we are to answer the second question, we must turn to official Latter-day Saints doctrine and check it out against historic, biblical and creedal Christianity. We will start to do this in chapter 6, but first, in the next few chapters, we will consider its origins.

TIP:

Rather than assuming you know what Mormons believe, ask them questions. Have them define their terms. This will aid you in two important ways. Firstly, it will stop them from sounding Christian. Secondly, you will hear what the individual Mormon you are speaking to believes. Unlike the Jehovah's Witnesses, who generally believe and answer things identically, Mormons will differ in many of their beliefs.

3

JOSEPH SMITH – THE PROPHET OF THE RESTORATION

No man can accept Jesus Christ as the Savior of the world, no man can accept this as His church, the Church of Jesus Christ, unless he can accept Joseph Smith as God's mouthpiece and the restorer of His work in these latter days (Harold B. Lee).[5]

Joseph Smith, the Prophet and Seer of the Lord, has done more, save Jesus only, for the salvation of men in this world, than any other man that lived in it (Doctrine and Covenants 135:3).

Young Joseph Smith made an astonishing claim. He said that, in the spring of 1820, God the Father and Jesus Christ appeared to him as he prayed in a grove of trees near his home in western New York. This event is known, in Mormonism, as the 'First Vision'.

The validity of this First Vision is integral to all that is the Church of Jesus Christ of Latter-day Saints – a fact that has not been lost on Mormon leaders throughout its history. Joseph Fielding Smith, who served as the tenth President of the Mormon Church, said:

> *Mormonism, as it is called, must stand or fall on the story of Joseph Smith. He was either a prophet of God, divinely called, properly appointed and commissioned, or he was one of the biggest frauds this world has ever seen. There is no middle ground.*[6]

Gordon B. Hinckley, the fifteenth President of the Mormon Church, agrees:

> *Our whole strength rests on the validity of that vision. It either occurred or it did not occur. If it did not, then this work is a fraud ... upon*

> *that unique and wonderful experience stands the validity of this church.*[7]

WHO WAS JOSEPH SMITH?

Joseph Smith Junior was born on 23 December 1805 in Sharon, Vermont. He was one of eleven children born to Joseph Smith Senior and Lucy Mack Smith. Around the age of ten, Joseph and his family moved to Palmyra, New York.

Joseph claimed that between the ages of twelve and fifteen he became interested in spiritual things and the state of his own soul. In the official First Vision account we read:

> *In the early 1800s in the United States there was great excitement about religion. Joseph's family members had joined different churches, but Joseph was unsure which one he should join.*
>
> *When Joseph was 14 years old, he was inspired by James 1:5, which promises, 'If any of you lack wisdom, let him ask of God, that giveth to all men liberally, and upbraideth not; and it shall be given him.' Joseph determined to pray to know which church he should join and to ask for forgiveness of his sins.*

When Joseph knelt to offer up the desires of his heart, a dark power overcame him. It bound his tongue as thick darkness gathered around him. Joseph exerted all his power to call upon God.

He described what happened next:

'I saw a pillar of light exactly over my head, above the brightness of the sun, which descended gradually until it fell upon me.

... When the light rested upon me I saw two Personages, whose brightness and glory defy all description, standing above me in the air. One of them spake unto me, calling me by name and said, pointing to the other – This is My Beloved Son. Hear Him!'

At the moment the light appeared, Joseph felt delivered from the enemy that had held him bound. Joseph felt great joy and love for several days after.

During the vision, Joseph asked which church was correct, and Jesus Christ answered, telling Joseph not to join any of them. The Lord explained that the churches of the day believed 'in incorrect doctrines and that none of them was acknowledged of God as His Church and kingdom'.

> *The First Vision marked the beginning of the Restoration of the gospel of Jesus Christ in this last dispensation. Joseph Smith was chosen to be the Lord's prophet in the latter days. Over time, the Lord restored His authority and Church through Joseph Smith. God's children were again blessed with revelation through prophets called of God, just as they were in biblical times. Revelation continues to this day through each of God's chosen prophets who have succeeded Joseph Smith.*[8]

The reason I said this is the 'official First Vision account' is because there are actually nine First Vision accounts, all of which are recorded in various writings of the Church of Jesus Christ of Latter-day Saints. There are numerous differences in these accounts including Joseph Smith's age, the location of the event, his reasons for going to pray and the things he saw. Of all these perhaps the most surprising is his confusion about how many personages he saw. In 1831–1832 he claimed that he saw the Lord. In an 1835 communication he claimed he saw one personage. Then in 1840 he claimed that he saw two glorious personages (the Father and the Son).

QUESTIONS FOR MORMON MISSIONARIES

Why did it take Joseph twelve years to write about that First Vision? Also, in 1832 Joseph wrote that the 'Lord' appeared to him and forgave him his sin. Why did he not mention then that the Father and Son (as in the official First Vision account) had appeared to him? That is like telling someone you once met Prince Charles, and then telling the same person eight years later that you now remembered the Queen was there as well!

It is hard to account for the differences in the First Vision accounts. It is certainly inconceivable that the Father and the Son (the two personages) appeared to Joseph but that he forgot or got it wrong.

THE 'SO-CALLED' APOSTATE CHURCH

According to the Church of Jesus Christ of Latter-day Saints, the purpose for the Father and Son appearing to Joseph was to restore the true church through him. He was chosen to be the Prophet of the Restoration.

QUESTIONS FOR MORMON MISSIONARIES

When did the church become so totally apostate that it needed to be restored? How does this accord with Jesus' words in the Bible: 'I will build my church, and the gates of hell shall not prevail against it' (Matthew 16:18)?

The official First Vision account contains these words, allegedly spoken by 'the Lord' to Joseph Smith:

> *During the vision, Joseph asked which church was correct, and Jesus Christ answered, telling Joseph not to join any of them.* The Lord explained that the churches of the day believed 'in incorrect doctrines and

that none of them was acknowledged of God as His Church and kingdom' (my emphasis).

Now let's compare this to Joseph's recollection of the First Vision as recorded in the LDS *History of the Church*:

> *My object in going to inquire of the Lord was to know which of all the sects was right, that I might know which to join. No sooner, therefore, did I get possession of myself, so as to be able to speak, than I asked the personages who stood above me in the light, which of all the sects was right – and which I should join.* I was answered that I must join none of them, for they were all wrong, and the personage who addressed me said that all their creeds were an abomination in His sight: that those professors were all corrupt … (my emphasis).[9]

I am sure you will have noticed the deliberate 'dumbing down', in the official account, of what the Lord apparently said to Joseph about the churches. Though the Church of Jesus

Christ of Latter-day Saints is reluctant to say so, the truth is that it *does* believe that mainstream Christianity is corrupt and an abomination. It believes itself to be the one and only true church on the planet.

JOSEPH THE PROPHET

Within the Church of Jesus Christ of Latter-day Saints, Joseph Smith is revered as a Prophet of God:

> ... I know he was God's prophet, chosen to restore the gospel of Jesus Christ in these latter days ... *May our lives reflect the knowledge we have that God lives, that Jesus Christ is His Son, that Joseph Smith was a prophet, and that we are led today by another prophet of God – even President Gordon B. Hinckley (Thomas S. Monson,* my emphasis*).*[10]

A few years ago, whilst doing outreach to the Church of Jesus Christ of Latter-day Saints in Utah, I was invited to visit a Mormon home. I remember thinking how it was like visiting the home of a Roman Catholic because there were religious pictures everywhere. But instead of pictures of the Pope, Mary and St Peter's Basilica hanging on the wall, this Mormon home had pictures of Joseph Smith, Thomas Monson (the President at the time) and the Salt Lake City Temple.

Just as the Roman Catholic will revere – and in some instances come dangerously close to worshipping – the Pope, Mormons do likewise with Joseph Smith. They even sing a hymn dedicated to their founding prophet. Here are the first two verses:

> *Praise to the man who communed*
> *with Jehovah!*
> *Jesus anointed that Prophet and Seer.*
> *Blessed to open the last dispensation,*
> *Kings shall extol him, and nations revere*
> *Praise to his mem'ry, he died as a martyr;*
> *Honored and blest be his ever great name!*
> *Long shall his blood, which was shed*
> *by assassins,*
> *Plead unto heav'n while the earth lauds*
> *his fame (William W. Phelps).*[11]

If that hymn doesn't quite convey the esteem Mormons have for Joseph, how about these words from his successor Brigham Young:

> *From the day that the Priesthood was taken from the earth to the winding-up scene of all things, every man and woman must have the certificate of Joseph Smith, junior, as a passport to their entrance into the mansion where God and Christ are – I with you and you with me. I cannot go there without his consent. He holds the keys of that kingdom for the last dispensation ...*[12]

Mormons may disagree upon numerous things, but the person and importance of Joseph Smith isn't one of them. This is because they are taught that without accepting that Joseph Smith was a prophet, who was called by God to restore the apostate church, they cannot live eternally with Heavenly Father and Jesus Christ.

QUESTIONS FOR MORMON MISSIONARIES

Ask the missionaries if they believe that Joseph Smith was a prophet. They will certainly say yes. Then ask them whether, as a prophet, Joseph ever prophesied something that came to pass. If they say yes, ask them what it was and did it happen. If they say no, or they do not know, ask them to read to you from Doctrine and Covenants 84:1–5. This revelation to Joseph Smith declares that the New Jerusalem and the temple will be built in Missouri.

Once they have read this revelation, ask whether this happened. The answer is 'No' – they did not build a temple in Missouri in Joseph's lifetime.

Next, ask whether this was a false prophecy. The answer is 'Yes'. The Bible is very clear about this: '… when a prophet speaks in the name of the LORD, if the word does not come to pass or come true, that is a word that the LORD has not spoken' (Deuteronomy 18:22).

4

THE BOOK OF MORMON

> *I told the brethren that the Book of Mormon was the most correct of any book on earth, and the keystone of our religion, and a man would get nearer to God by abiding by its precepts, than by any other book (Joseph Smith).*[13]
>
> *HELLO! Would you like to change religions?! I have a free book written by Jesus! (The Book of Mormon).*[14]

I had just seen the musical *The Book of Mormon* and was stepping out of the theatre when I saw them. They were lying in wait for unsuspecting theatregoers. These young adults with bright smiling faces were holding out blue books. Yes, you guessed right – they were Mormon missionaries.

Though the musical does nothing but seriously ridicule Mormonism, the Church of Jesus Christ of Latter-day Saints sees this as an opportunity to introduce the public to their Church. They boldly declare, 'You have seen the musical, now read the Book!' as they give the Book of Mormon to whomever will receive it.

TIP:

If the musical *The Book of Mormon* is being performed at a theatre near you, why not go along and share the gospel with the missionaries that will be outside. You may also want to discuss with those leaving the theatre what they thought about it and have some gospel tracts to give away.

Most sought to avoid these Mormons but I made a beeline towards them, eager to receive my free book. I asked the missionary sisters at the table why they were giving out the Book of Mormon and not the Bible. They replied that they were happy to give out Bibles as well, but they only had the Book of Mormon with them (as is always the case). However, perhaps the answer to my question really lies in what their teaching has to say about the Bible:

> *… for behold, they have taken away from the gospel of the Lamb many parts which are plain and most precious; and also many covenants of the Lord have they taken away.*
>
> *… because of the many plain and precious things which have been taken out of the book, which were plain unto the understanding of the children of men, according to the plainness which is in the Lamb of God because of these things which are taken away out of the gospel of the Lamb, an exceeding great many do stumble, yea, insomuch that Satan hath great power over them (1 Nephi 13:26, 29).*
>
> *We believe the Bible to be the word of God as far as it is translated correctly; we also believe the Book of Mormon to be the word of God (Article 8).*

Though they claim the Bible has worth, they value the Book of Mormon more, as Ezra Taft Benson, their thirteenth President, explains:

> *All scripture is not of equal value. The book that is the 'keystone of our religion' and that will get a man 'nearer to God by abiding by its precepts, than by any other book' needs to be studied constantly.*[15]
>
> *Of the four great standard works of the Church – the Bible, the Book of Mormon, the Doctrine and Covenants, and the Pearl of Great Price – I would particularly urge you to read again and again the Book of Mormon and ponder and apply its teachings.*[16]

TIP:

Ask the Mormon missionaries where the Bible has not been translated correctly. They usually have no idea. Instead, they work on the premise that wherever the Bible contradicts the Book of Mormon or Mormon teaching, it must have been translated incorrectly.

THE 'KEYSTONE OF OUR RELIGION'

The Book of Mormon is a difficult read. Curiously, it is written in King James English. A person well acquainted with the contents of the Bible will note that there are large portions of the Book of Mormon that are lifted directly from the Bible. However, though its content sounds something like the Bible, it speaks of unfamiliar places and peoples.

According to Joseph Smith, he was directed by an angel to the discovery of what was to become the Book of Mormon:

> *He called me by name, and said he was a messenger sent from the presence of God to me, and his name was Moroni … He said there was a book deposited, written upon gold plates, giving an account of former inhabitants of this continent, and the source from where they sprang. He also said that the fulness of the everlasting Gospel was contained in it, as delivered by the Saviour to the ancient inhabitants.*[17]

The location of these plates was the Hill Cumorah (which is claimed to be near the town of Manchester, New York). Upon finding the plates, Joseph Smith needed to translate them as they were written in an unknown language called Reformed Egyptian. This is what the Church of Jesus Christ of Latter-day Saints says about the translation process:

> *Joseph Smith dictated the words of the translation to scribes, mostly Oliver Cowdery. Because Joseph was translating a completely unknown language, he needed to rely on the Lord. One way the Lord helped was to provide physical instruments to aid Joseph in translating. Witnesses said Joseph looked into the instruments and that words appeared to him in English. The translation instruments included the 'interpreters' or 'Urim and Thummim' – two clear stones fastened in a metal rim so that Joseph could look through them. These had been given to Joseph along with the plates. Another instrument Joseph used was a 'seer stone' that he would look into, often by placing it in a hat. Joseph had found this stone earlier and had used it to*

find hidden or lost things. He used both the interpreters and the seer stone as he translated, always relying on the inspiration of heaven.

The translation of the Book of Mormon was truly miraculous and was done 'by the gift and power of God'.[18]

TIP:

Ask the Mormon missionaries why there are no maps in the Book of Mormon. The reason is because there is no archaeological, geographical or historical evidence for anything the book claims. Unlike the Bible, which is greatly supported by external evidence, the peoples, places and accounts of the Book of Mormon are completely unfounded.

COMING TO AMERICA

The Book of Mormon gets its name from an ancient prophet named 'Mormon' who compiled the writings and sayings of a people who lived in the Americas from around 600 BC – AD 422. The story centres around God's dealings with these peoples.

Mormon passed his writings on to his son Moroni, who added a few things himself before burying the plates on a hillside. It was a now glorified Moroni who, in 1823, visited Joseph Smith to lead him to the plates.

The Book of Mormon reveals that a group of Israelites (the Lehites) travelled from Jerusalem in 600 BC and settled in the Americas. Once there, these people separated into two people groups who often warred against each other – the Nephites and the Lamanites. The Book of Mormon not only tells the story of these peoples, but also recounts how Jesus, after his death and resurrection, visited them. Afterwards, there was peace amongst all the inhabitants, but eventually the fighting resumed. The Nephites were finally destroyed, with the victorious Lamanites becoming the forebears of the Native Americans.

It is this book that Mormons challenge people to pray about in order to receive spiritual confirmation of its authenticity.

5

THE WORD OF WISDOM

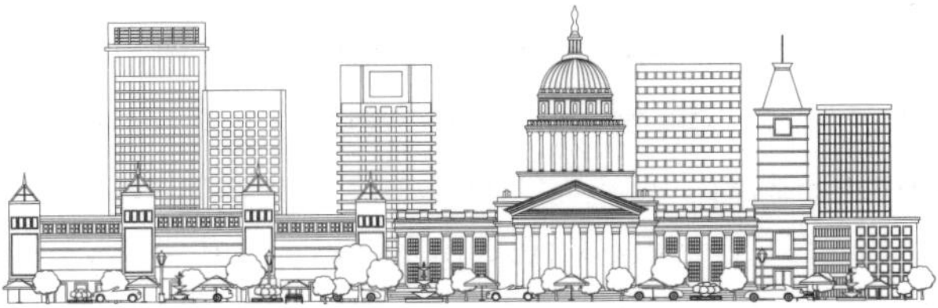

But says one, 'If I am offered a cup of tea or a cup of coffee I cannot refuse it.' Then, according to the word of the Lord, you are too weak to be a Latter-day Saint (Joseph Smith).[19]

I love cranberry juice, but I'm not a coffee drinker – as a Mormon, I avoid caffeine (Donny Osmond).

One thing people tend to know about Mormons is that they do not drink tea or coffee, but they have no idea why. Where does this injunction come from? The answer is to be found in the Word of Wisdom, their law of health.

THE ORIGIN OF THIS HEALTH CODE

It is claimed that what is known as the Word of Wisdom came from a revelation given by God to Joseph Smith on 27 February 1833. It is recorded in section 89 of the Mormon Scripture known as Doctrine and Covenants. This speaks of what is good and bad for the human body and therefore is seen as a health code for Mormons.

God told Joseph that the following is good:

- Fruits and wholesome herbs, including vegetables, which should be used 'with prudence and thanksgiving' (89:10–11)
- The flesh 'of beasts and of the fowls of the air', which is 'to be used sparingly' (89:12–13)
- Grains such as wheat, rice and oats, which are 'the staff of life' (89:14–17)

God told Joseph that the following is bad:

- Alcoholic drinks (89:5–7)
- Tobacco (89:8)
- Tea and coffee (89:9)

Joseph continued: 'The Lord promises increased health, wisdom, knowledge, and protection to those who obey the Word of Wisdom' (89:18–21).

It is interesting to note that Doctrine and Covenants 89:9 says, 'And again, hot drinks are not for the body or belly,' but does not define what is meant by hot drinks. I often agree to meet Mormon missionaries in coffee shops. Whilst refusing tea or coffee, so far they have always accepted my offer to buy them a 'healthy' hot chocolate, with cream and marshmallows. Are they breaking the Word of Wisdom? Apparently not, as latter-day prophets have taught that the term 'hot drinks', as written in this verse, refers only to tea and coffee.

TIP:

Point out to Mormon missionaries that 'tea' refers to the process not the product. It is an infusion of leaves. Can a Mormon drink an infusion of mint?

OPEN TO REVISION, BUT ESSENTIAL TO KEEP

Here we find this principle in Mormonism: modern prophets have the right to change, amend, refute, interpret and/or reveal new revelations. Of course, none would ever dare remove or usurp the teachings and revelations of the Prophet Joseph Smith.

Though breaking the Word of Wisdom can be repented of and forgiven, failing to keep it can have eternal consequences, as Joseph Fielding Smith explains:

> *SALVATION AND A CUP OF TEA. You cannot neglect little things. 'Oh, a cup of tea is such a little thing. It is so little; surely it doesn't amount to much; surely the Lord will forgive me if I drink a cup of tea.' Yes, he will forgive you, because he is going to forgive every man who repents; but, my brethren, if you drink coffee or tea, or take tobacco, are you letting a cup of tea or a little tobacco stand in the road and bar you from the celestial kingdom of God, where you might otherwise have received a fulness of glory?*[20]

Can a cup of tea keep a person from the celestial kingdom of God and the receiving of the fullness of glory? In Mormon theology the answer is yes. But what do they mean by the 'celestial kingdom' and 'fulness of glory'? To understand that, we must now begin to look at Mormon doctrine, starting with the Mormon Plan of Salvation.

QUESTIONS FOR MORMON MISSIONARIES

Can returning to Heavenly Father really be dependent on what we do or do not drink? Where in the Bible does it say that if you believe on the Lord Jesus Christ, you will be saved, so long as you don't have a cup of tea? Ask them to read Mark 7:18–19: 'Do you not see that whatever goes into a person from outside cannot defile him, since it enters not his heart but his stomach, and is expelled?' Then ask them what Jesus is teaching. Next, have them read Romans 10:9: 'if you confess with your mouth that Jesus is Lord and believe in your heart that God raised him from the dead, you will be saved.' What does that teach?

THE PLAN OF SALVATION

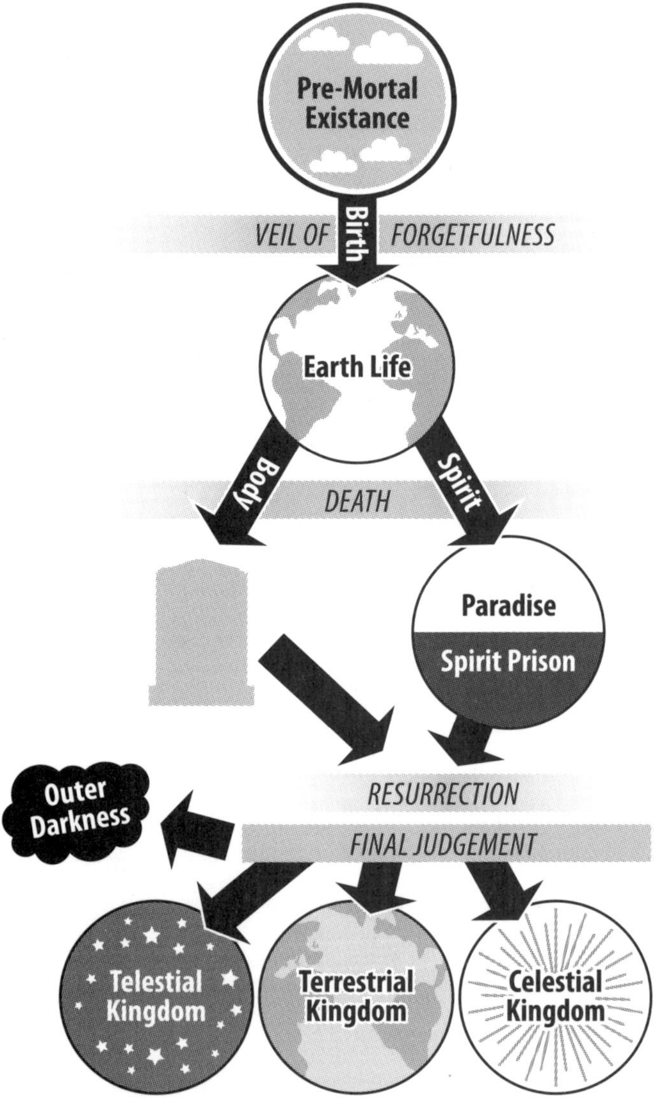

6

THE PLAN OF SALVATION

If you meet Mormon missionaries with the intention of going through their lessons, you will eventually hear about the Plan of Salvation (also known as the Plan of Happiness).

The Plan of Salvation gives an overview of God's plan to save humanity from sin and its consequences. You will be told about how we all pre-existed as Heavenly Father's spirit children before we were born. The reason we don't remember this is because on our journey from the spirit world to birth, we had to pass through the Veil of Forgetfulness. (I don't remember doing that!)

We leave the pre-mortal world and come to earth to live out our plan of salvation. Every spirit child needs to be born into mortality so that they may progress and hopefully one day return to Heavenly Father. That is why Mormons have large families – so that those spirits who are waiting to be born will be born in a Mormon family.

Whilst in your mortal state, you have what they call agency, that is freedom to make decisions. Your choices may be wise or unwise. However, it is not just decisions made in mortality that will determine your eternal destiny. You also have a chance to make the right choices post-mortem. Let's consider this step by step.

SECOND CHANCE?

Mormons teach that when we die, our bodies go to the ground and our spirits go to the spirit world. There we find two sections – spirit paradise and spirit prison. If you died a faithful Mormon, you will enter paradise, but if you died a non-Mormon, you will enter prison (also known as hell). However, neither of these locations are the final destination of the individuals who find themselves there. Your final estate will be determined at the future resurrection.

Fortunately, even if you find yourself in spirit prison, that need not be the end of your story. Whilst there, you will be visited by Mormon 'spirit' missionaries (there is no escape) who will offer you, once again, the opportunity to accept the laws and ordinances of the Mormon gospel.

TIP:

The Bible teaches that there is no second chance: 'And just as it is appointed for man to die once, and after that comes judgment …' (Hebrews 9:27).

If you accept the Mormon gospel whilst in spirit prison, you will be released and allowed to enter spirit paradise, but something else needs to happen first.

BAPTISM

Mormons teach that if you are to be saved in the fullest sense – that is, you are to receive the promised fullness of glory – baptism is a necessary requirement. And, as I mentioned previously, you must be baptised by those with priesthood authority. So, if you decide to embrace Mormonism in spirit prison, you need also to be baptised, but here lies a couple of problems. Firstly, you can't be baptised because you don't have a resurrected physical body, which is essential for this rite. Secondly, there is apparently no water in spirit prison! How can these problems be overcome? This is where Mormon temples come into play.

TEMPLES

There is no doubt that Mormon temples are impressive looking buildings. These large, glistening white structures often have beautifully manicured gardens. If there is any doubt as to who the building belongs to, look up. If you see an angel (Moroni) blowing a trumpet on top of the building, it is a Mormon temple.

The temple is not where ordinary Mormons go to worship – they do that at local buildings called 'meeting houses' or 'ward buildings'. Rather, the temple is a House of the Lord, where God especially dwells and where special ordinances are performed. One of those ordinances is called 'Baptism for the Dead'.

It has been said that if you want to research your ancestry, you should go to the Church of Jesus Christ of Latter-day Saints. They have extensive genealogical records which are used, unbeknown to most people, to baptise the dead in their temples. As Mormons do not know who may accept the Mormon gospel in spirit prison, they baptise by proxy for everyone they can.

Baptism by proxy is performed for those who have passed from this life as non-Mormons but now accept the Mormon gospel. Once a stand-in person is baptised for them in the temple, the person is released from spirit prison and upgraded to paradise.

Mormons will point to 1 Corinthians 15:29 as proof that baptism for the dead is biblical: 'Else what shall they do which are baptized for the dead, if the dead rise not at all? why are they then baptized for the dead?' (KJV) Cults will often pull verses out of their context to promote obscure doctrine. Though commentators may put forth different ideas to what the Apostle Paul was talking about here, they all agree that Paul is neither advocating baptism for the dead nor claiming it to be something practised by the early church.

When 1 Corinthians 15 is read in context, it is clear that Paul is addressing the believers as 'brethren' in verse 1. Throughout he uses the words 'you', 'we' and 'us', except in one place. In verse 29 he says 'what shall *they* do which are baptized for the dead ... why are *they* then baptized for the dead?' (my emphasis).

It is reasonable to assume that Paul is speaking of those who are not of the brethren of the Lord Jesus Christ. Paul could have been addressing a practice connected to the area of Corinth. However, as the Bible nowhere else mentions this practice, nor was it a practice of the early church, we can rightly say that it has never been Christian practice.

It is also worth asking Mormons to read some verses from the Book of Mormon which teach that today is the day of salvation:

> *Yea, I would that ye would come forth and harden not your hearts any longer; for behold,*

now is the time and the day of your salvation; and therefore, if ye will repent and harden not your hearts, immediately shall the great plan of redemption be brought about unto you.

For behold, this life is the time for men to prepare to meet God; yea, behold the day of this life is the day for men to perform their labors.

And now, as I said unto you before, as ye have had so many witnesses, therefore, I beseech of you that ye do not procrastinate the day of your repentance until the end; for after this day of life, which is given us to prepare for eternity, behold, if we do not improve our time while in this life, then cometh the night of darkness wherein there can be no labor performed (Alma 34:31–33).

TIP:

While Mormons believe that God especially dwells in their temples, the Bible tells us that this is not true: 'the Most High does not dwell in houses made by hands' (Acts 7:48).

ALL SAVED?

> *All mankind shall be saved in one or another kingdom. Even the wicked, after they have paid the debt shall be admitted into the Telestial Kingdom, the glory of which surpasseth all understanding, but where God and his Christ shall never come, worlds without end. Thus God has provided for the salvation of all his children excepting only the sons of Perdition, those who shed innocent blood and who deny the Son after the Father has revealed him (Rulon S. Wells).*[21]

According to Mormonism, almost everyone will be saved, but they will not find themselves in the same place. When the final judgment takes place, nearly all will be allocated a place in one of three kingdoms.

The lowest of these is named the Telestial Kingdom, which the quote above claims has 'glory of which surpasseth all understanding'. This, according to Mormon doctrine, will be the final resting place of the most wicked. So, for example, Mormons believe that Hitler and all his Nazi co-conspirators will be there. Once the wicked have 'paid their debt', they will be allowed to live in glorious freedom, the only downside for them being that they will never get a visit from Heavenly Father and Jesus. (I'm not too sure the likes of Hitler would be too bothered about that.)

Those who are not as bad as the Nazis but not as good as the Mormons will be given access to the middle kingdom known as the Terrestrial Kingdom: 'Those who have been decent and upright and who have lived respectable and good lives will go to a terrestrial kingdom whose glory is as the moon' (Spencer W. Kimball).[22]

The Terrestrial Kingdom will be home to, amongst others, Christians who don't belong to the Church of Jesus Christ of Latter-day Saints, as well as lukewarm Mormons. There is good news and bad news for the inhabitants of this kingdom. The good news is that Jesus will occasionally visit, but the bad news is that, like one who has been denied parental rights, Heavenly Father can never come to see you.

The final kingdom, which is exclusively for faithful Latter-day Saints, is called the Celestial Kingdom. This is where Heavenly Father and Jesus abide. Only those who have been obedient to all the laws and ordinances of the Mormon gospel will gain entrance into this kingdom.

In Mormon doctrine, therefore, whilst nearly all will be saved, only a few will reach exaltation (the highest possible level of salvation). It is in the Celestial Kingdom that families are reunited and that marriages will continue for time and eternity. Some will even go on to become a God, being given their own planet to rule over.

You will have noticed that I kept saying that 'nearly all' will be saved. That is because there is a final place called Outer Darkness, which is reserved for Satan and his minions, and for those who the Mormons call the 'sons of Perdition':

> *There is another class of sons of perdition. This class is composed of all those who have known the power of God in this mortal life and then, having* full knowledge of the power and purposes of God, *rebel against him, putting Jesus Christ to open shame (Joseph Fielding Smith,* his emphasis*).*[23]

This basically means that, according to Mormon doctrine, all ex-Mormons – even those who have left Mormonism and come to a real living faith in the Lord Jesus Christ – will find themselves in Outer Darkness.

The chief end in Mormonism is to return to Heavenly Father. To do this one has to follow all the edicts of the Church of Jesus Christ of Latter-day Saints. If you do so, you could one day find yourself to be a God.

7

GOD THE MAN

These ideas are incomprehensible to some, but they are simple. It is the first principle of the gospel to know for a certainty the character of God, and to know that we may converse with Him as one man converses with another, and that He was once a man like us; yea, that God Himself, the Father of us all, dwelt on an earth, the same as Jesus Christ Himself did; and I will show it from the Bible (Joseph Smith).[24]

Official doctrine of the Church of Jesus Christ of Latter-day Saints teaches that 'God himself was once as we are now, and is an exalted man, and sits enthroned in yonder heavens!' They believe that God was once a sinful man existing on 'an earth'. After working out his own Plan of Salvation, he received the highest reward: he became a God. He is now God of our planet. Known by Mormons as Heavenly Father, he – along with Heavenly Mother – populated the spirit world with spirit children. (The doctrine of a Heavenly Mother is an established belief among Latter-day Saints, though there is no record of a formal revelation to Joseph Smith about this.) The Plan of Salvation was then set in motion on our planet.

You can be forgiven for thinking this teaching sounds more like a plot from a science fiction film rather than biblical Christianity.

QUESTIONS FOR MORMON MISSIONARIES

If you believe that God was once a sinful man, do you worship an exalted sinful man?

I think it is fair to say that the Mormon God is not the God of the Bible. There are many problems with their teaching. First and foremost, it is contradicted by both the Bible and the Book of Mormon. You could use the following dialogue to show them this problem.

QUESTIONS FOR MORMON MISSIONARIES

You: Do you believe in Moroni 8:18 in the Book of Mormon?

Missionaries: Yes, we do.

You: Can you please read it to me?

Missionaries: Of course. It is: 'God is not a partial God, neither a changeable being; but he is unchangeable from all eternity to all eternity.'

You: That sounds very much like a verse in the Bible. Please read Psalm 90:2.

Missionaries: 'Before the mountains were brought forth, or ever thou hadst formed the earth and the world, even from everlasting to everlasting, thou art God' (KJV).

You: What do these verses teach us about God? (If they don't point to the following,

CONTINUE ↓

explain that they show firstly that God has been God from all eternity, and secondly that God has never changed and is not a changeable being.) Do you agree that this is what these two verses say about God?

Missionaries: Yes.

You: Have you heard of the King Follett sermon preached by Joseph Smith? (Some will have, some won't, whilst others will have but won't admit it.) This is what Joseph Smith said: 'God himself was once as we are now, and is an exalted man, and sits enthroned in yonder heavens!' Do you agree with Joseph that God was once a man?

(This should cause the missionaries some dissonance. The Bible and the Book of Mormon say that God has always been God, yet Joseph contradicts both by claiming that God was once a man who became God.)

You: Do you believe the Bible and the Book of Mormon *or* do you believe Joseph?

MAN CAN BECOME GOD

Following on from their conviction that God was once a man is their belief that they too can become a God. If they follow the Mormon Plan of Salvation to the letter, they too are heading for Godhood. This belief is summed up by what is known as the Mormon couplet, penned by the fifth President of the Church, Lorenzo Snow: 'As man is God once was, as God is man may be.' Latter-day Saints missionaries believe that, with total obedience, they too can reach Godhood.

TIP:

As you engage in discussions with Mormon missionaries, it is worth being aware of something called cognitive dissonance. In the field of psychology, cognitive dissonance occurs when a person holds two or more contradictory beliefs, ideas or values, or participates in an action that goes against one of these three, resulting in them experiencing psychological stress.

WILL THE REAL GOD PLEASE STAND UP

It is important not to belittle the beliefs of those with whom we disagree, but rather lovingly to point out why we don't agree with them. Where possible we would want to point them to where Mormon doctrine is at odds with the Bible. On this particular topic we could ask them to read the following verses:

> *'You are my witnesses,' declares the Lord, 'and my servant whom I have chosen, that you may know and believe me, and understand that I am he. Before me no God was formed, nor shall there be any after me. I, I am the* LORD, *and besides me there is no saviour (Isaiah 43:10–11).*
>
> *Thus says the Lord, the King of Israel and his Redeemer, the* LORD *of hosts: 'I am the first and I am the last; besides me there is no god' (Isaiah 44:6).*
>
> *Fear not, nor be afraid; have I not told you from of old and declared it? And you are my witnesses! Is there a God besides me? There is no Rock; I know not any (Isaiah 44:8).*

Point out that these verses clearly contradict Mormon doctrine, so any Latter-day Saint must make a choice: the Bible or Mormonism.

TIP:

Often, when backed into a corner, Mormon missionaries will 'bear their testimony'. Beginning with 'I believe …' they will declare what they believe about themselves. When using the verses above from Isaiah, tell them that these words are God's testimony to us about himself.

When sharing these same verses, Mormons will also be prone to saying that they are talking about there being only one God over this planet. Ask them where in the Bible it talks about other planets with other Gods.

Article 8 of the Church of Jesus Christ of Latter-day Saints declares: 'We believe the bible to be the word of God as far as it is translated correctly; we also believe the book of Mormon to be the word of God.' Note the difference here between how they regard the Bible and the Book of Mormon. Therefore, be prepared when sharing Bible verses with missionaries that they may say they are not sure the Bible has been translated correctly.

TIP:

It is always worth using the same Scripture version as them: the King James Version. This will help to stop them saying that different versions prove that the Bible is unreliable.

So the God of Mormonism is not the God of the Bible, but surely we believe in the same Jesus – don't we? That brings us to the next chapter.

8

THE JESUS OF MORMONISM

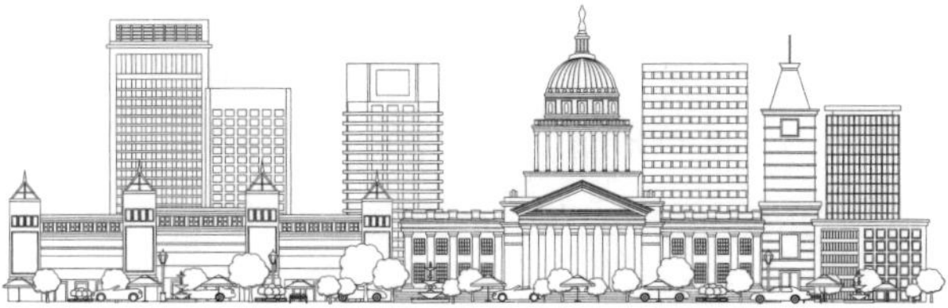

In bearing testimony of Jesus Christ, President Hinckley spoke of those outside the Church who say Latter-day Saints 'do not believe in the traditional Christ'. 'No, I don't. The traditional Christ of whom they speak is not the Christ of whom I speak' (Church News).[25]

Though Mormon missionaries will be adamant that they are Christians because they believe in Jesus, we need to consider who their Jesus is.

THE JESUS OF THE LATTER-DAY SAINTS

The Latter-day Saints believe that the traditional Jesus is a distorted Jesus who is the product of tradition and church councils. In contrast, their 'real' Jesus was revealed through the restoration.

> **TIP:**
>
> When someone says that they believe in Jesus, we should always ask: Which one?[26] The Apostle Paul himself warned Christians to be on their guard '… if someone comes and proclaims another Jesus than the one we proclaimed' (2 Corinthians 11:4).

The following quotes reveal something of the Mormon Jesus:

> *Jesus Christ is the Son of Elohim both as spiritual and bodily offspring; that is to say, Elohim is literally the Father of the spirit of Jesus Christ and also of the body in which Jesus Christ performed His mission in the flesh … (James Talmage).*[27]

Even Christ himself was not perfect at first; he received not a fulness at first, but he received grace for grace, and he continued to receive more and more until he received a fulness (Joseph Fielding Smith).[28]

Long before you were born a program was developed by your creators … The principle personalities in this great drama were a Father Elohim, perfect in wisdom, judgment, and person, and two sons, Lucifer and Jehovah (Spencer W. Kimball).[29]

QUESTIONS FOR MORMON MISSIONARIES

Do you believe that the human Jesus was produced by Heavenly Father having sexual relations with Mary? Though they are often reluctant to talk about this, this is what Mormon doctrine teaches.

Mormons believe that while Heavenly Mother was the mother of Jesus in pre-mortality, the spirit Jesus had to be born as all humans are in order to come to earth. It has been taught that this happened by

CONTINUE ↓

Heavenly Father visiting Mary and having a sexual relationship with her.

TIP:

Be aware that Mormons also call Heavenly Father 'Elohim' and also call Jesus 'Jehovah'.

The Mormons teach that Heavenly Father had a plan of salvation and two candidates applied for the job: Jesus and his spirit brother, Lucifer. Jesus suggested that mortals should continue to have agency (freedom of choice). Lucifer wanted to save everyone by taking away their agency and therefore their freedom to sin against God. However, agency was fundamental to God's plan, and Jesus promised to honour it. Lucifer wanted instead God's throne and power. There was a war in heaven and the outcome is recorded in Revelation 12.

We learn more about the Mormon Jesus through these writings:

> *Christ attained Godhood while yet in pre-existence, he too stood as a God to the other spirits, but this relationship was not the same one of personal parenthood that prevailed between the Father and his offspring (Bruce R. McConkie).*[30]
>
> *Jesus became a God and reached His great state of understanding through consistent effort and continuous obedience to all the Gospel truths and universal laws (Milton R. Hunter).*[31]

The official teaching of the Church of Jesus Christ of Latter-day Saints clearly reveals a *different* Jesus to what the Bible teaches is true. The Bible tells us that Jesus has eternally been God and created all things:

> *Jesus Christ is the same yesterday and today and for ever (Hebrews 13:8).*

> *In the beginning was the Word, and the Word was with God, and the Word was God (John 1:1).*

> *All things were made through him, and without him was not any thing made that was made (John 1:3).*
>
> *For by him were all things created, in heaven and on earth, visible and invisible, whether thrones or dominions or rulers or authorities – all things were created through him and for him. And he is before all things, and in him all things hold together (Colossians 1:16–17).*

In contrast, the Mormon Jesus is not the eternal God, but rather was the offspring of Elohim (Heavenly Father). In his pre-existence before being born of Mary he was named Jehovah, and Lucifer is his spirit brother. He was conceived because of a physical relationship between Heavenly Father and Mary. He then became a God through 'consistent effort and continuous obedience to all the Gospel truths and universal laws'.

Considering these beliefs, former President Gordon B. Hinckley's words appear painfully inadequate: 'As a Church we have critics, many of them. They say we do not believe in the traditional Christ of Christianity. *There is some substance to what they say.*'[32]

The reality is that the Mormon Jesus is not the Jesus of orthodox, biblical Christianity. Theirs is 'another Jesus'.

THE MORMON JESUS IS NOT ENOUGH

The Bible says that Jesus is sufficient for our salvation. Jesus bore our sin. He is our righteousness. Our works add nothing to salvation because Jesus paid the price of all our sin.

Sadly, this is not how the Mormons view Jesus:

> *The Savior satisfied the demands of justice for those who repent of their sins and endeavor to keep all of His commandments when He stood in our place and suffered the penalty for our sins. This act is called the Atonement of Jesus Christ. Because of this selfless act, Christ can plead with the Father on our behalf. Heavenly Father can apply mercy, withhold punishment from us, and welcome us into His presence. Our Heavenly Father shows mercy when He forgives us of our sins and helps us return to dwell in His presence.*

However, Jesus did not eliminate our personal responsibility. He forgives our sins when we *accept Him, repent, and* obey His commandments. *Through Jesus Christ's Atonement and living the gospel we can enter the presence of our Heavenly Father permanently. We show that we accept Christ and that we have faith in Him by doing His will and keeping His commandments, including obeying the first principles and ordinances of the gospel (Preach My Gospel,* my emphasis*).*[33]

QUESTIONS FOR MORMON MISSIONARIES

Ask whether trusting in Jesus alone is enough to get back to Heavenly Father. If they answer 'Yes', then they are not being honest. Ask them what they must do to get back to Heavenly Father – they will have a long list!

If they answer 'No', then challenge them with a further question. Are they saying that Jesus' death and resurrection was not enough – but rather just a down

CONTINUE →

payment or a deposit – and that now we have to play our part, effectively paying the monthly instalments?

Then ask them to read the following Scriptures, which clearly show that Jesus bore our sin and is our righteousness, and therefore that our works add nothing to our salvation.

... who his own self bare our sins in his own body on the tree, that we, being dead to sins, should live unto righteousness: by whose stripes ye were healed (1 Peter 2:24, KJV*)*

For he hath made him to be sin for us, who knew no sin; that we might be made the righteousness of God in him (2 Corinthians 5:21, KJV*).*

For by grace are ye saved through faith; and that not of yourselves: it is the gift of God: not of works, lest any man should boast (Ephesians 2:8–9, KJV*).*

9

THE MORMON GODHEAD

We believe in God, the Eternal Father, and in His Son, Jesus Christ, and in the Holy Ghost (Article 1).

I have always declared God to be a distinct personage, Jesus Christ a separate and distinct personage from God the Father, and that the Holy Ghost was a distinct personage and a Spirit: and these three constitute three distinct personages and three Gods (Joseph Smith).[34]

TIP:

Be aware that, when asked, some Mormons will say that they believe in the Trinity, but you should not be fooled by this. Ask them to define their belief in the Trinity. This will expose their real belief to be tri-theism. They believe in a Godhead comprising of three separate Gods.

Mormons believe that the Trinity doctrine, as believed by the majority of Christendom, is at worst pagan and at best the product of centuries of debate. Therefore, they contend, it is not biblical but rather a human invention. In rejecting the Trinity, they follow the path of all non-Christian cults in denying a central tenet of the Christian faith.

On occasion I have been asked: Can a person be saved, yet deny the Trinity? My personal belief is no. Please know that I am not saying that a person must fully understand the triune nature of God, or even clearly articulate it, but any Christian must believe it. Rejecting the Trinity is rejecting God himself, the *one* God who has revealed himself to be Father, Son and Holy Spirit.

WHAT IS THE DOCTRINE OF THE TRINITY?

It is not within the scope of this book to do an exhaustive study on the Trinity. However, let me offer a definition of this doctrine from *The Forgotten Trinity* by James White – a book I highly recommend if you are interested in this subject area. James explains, '*Within the one Being that is God, there exists eternally three coequal and coeternal persons, namely, the Father, the Son, and the Holy Spirit.*'[35]

Though non-Christian cults would vociferously deny this definition of God, saying it is unbiblical, it is totally based upon biblical revelation and has been held to be true by believers throughout Christian history.

TIP:

You will often hear cult members say something like: 'The Trinity doctrine is a fourth-century invention.' Many cults claim that the doctrine of the Trinity originated at the Council of

CONTINUE ↓

Nicaea in AD 325. This is just not true. Their Mormon leaders (their ultimate authority) have told them that is the case, but they have never looked at the evidence for themselves. All the Council of Nicaea did was to ratify that which was already believed.

WHY BELIEVE IN THE TRINITY?

The short answer is because the Bible teaches it. Whilst the word 'Trinity' is not found in the Bible, that is not a problem. We use lots of words not found in the Bible to describe biblical truth, for example to describe God as 'omniscient', 'omnipresent', 'omnipotent' and 'benevolent'.

Below are a few of the numerous verses contained in the Bible that point to the truth of the triune nature of God:

> *And when Jesus was baptized, immediately he went up from the water, and behold, the heavens were opened to him, and he saw the Spirit of God descending like a dove and coming to rest on him (Matthew 3:16).*

Go therefore and make disciples of all nations, baptizing them in the name of the Father and of the Son and of the Holy Spirit (Matthew 28:19).

But the Helper, the Holy Spirit, whom the Father will send in my [Jesus'] name, he will teach you all things and bring to your remembrance all that I said to you (John 14:26).

But when the Helper comes, whom I [Jesus] will send to you from the Father, the Spirit of truth, who proceeds from the Father, he will bear witness about me (John 15:26).

And while staying with them he [Jesus] ordered them not to depart from Jerusalem, but to wait for the promise of the Father, which, he said, 'you heard from me' (Acts 1:4).

Being therefore exalted at the right hand of God, and having received from the Father the promise of the Holy Spirit, he [Jesus] has poured out this that you yourselves are seeing and hearing (Acts 2:33).

… you yourselves know … how God anointed Jesus of Nazareth with the Holy Spirit and with power. He went about doing good and healing all who were oppressed by the devil, for God was with him (Acts 10:37–38).

[Jesus] was declared to be the Son of God in power according to the Spirit of holiness by his resurrection from the dead, Jesus Christ our Lord (Romans 1:4).

You, however, are not in the flesh but in the Spirit, if in fact the Spirit of God dwells in you. Anyone who does not have the Spirit of Christ does not belong to him (Romans 8:9).

And such were some of you. But you were washed, you were sanctified, you were justified in the name of the Lord Jesus Christ and by the Spirit of our God (1 Corinthians 6:11).

The grace of the Lord Jesus Christ and the love of God and the fellowship of the Holy Spirit be with you all (2 Corinthians 13:14).

And because you are sons, God has sent the Spirit of his Son into our hearts, crying, 'Abba! Father!' (Galatians 4:6).

... that the God of our Lord Jesus Christ, the Father of glory, may give you the Spirit of wisdom and of revelation in the knowledge of him (Ephesians 1:17).

For through him we both have access in one Spirit to the Father (Ephesians 2:18).

In him [Jesus] you also are being built together into a dwelling place of God by the Spirit (Ephesians 2:22).

... whom he [the Holy Spirit] poured out on us richly through Jesus Christ our Saviour (Titus 3:6).

... how much more will the blood of Christ, who through the eternal Spirit offered himself without blemish to God, purify our conscience from dead works to serve the living God (Hebrews 9:14).

> *... according to the foreknowledge of God the Father, in the sanctification of the Spirit, for obedience to Jesus Christ and for sprinkling with his blood: May grace and peace be multiplied to you (1 Peter 1:2).*

In denying the triune nature of God, Mormons worship a different God.

TIP:

Ask Mormon missionaries to read some of the verses above and then to explain them to you. As you do so, remember this:

For the word of God is living and active, sharper than any two-edged sword, piercing to the division of soul and of spirit, of joints and of marrow, and discerning the thoughts and intentions of the heart (Hebrews 4:12).

10

THE IMPOSSIBLE GOSPEL

I have never been a fan of jigsaw puzzles. They frustrate me. I get that they can be relaxing for some, but trying to figure out what each individual piece is and where it fits in is not my idea of fun. As you look at the different pieces of the puzzle, they do not make sense until they are all placed together. Only then is the full picture revealed.

I want to suggest that the complete opposite applies to the beliefs of Mormonism. The pieces of the Mormon jigsaw puzzle only make sense when they are kept separate, for to join them together reveals a completely incoherent, nonsensical picture.

This can be seen when we put together all the pieces of the so-called Mormon gospel. In this chapter we shall work through a possible dialogue that we can have with Mormons to show them that their gospel does not make sense and cannot possibly save them. It is right to acknowledge that much of the following outline is the product of others trying to reach Mormons with the good news of Jesus.[36]

LOST AND FOUND

Mormons do not realise that they are lost spiritually, so we need to show them that they are – before we can then tell them how they can find true salvation. Our Mormon friends have been taught that the laws and ordinances of the Mormon Church make them righteous before a holy God. However, Paul, writing to the church in Galatia, points out that the true purpose of the law was different:

> *So then, the law was our guardian until Christ came, in order that we might be justified by faith (Galatians 3:24).*

Paul is teaching that the law, though given by God, cannot save anyone, but rather exposes our sinfulness. When we realise that we cannot keep the law, and therefore cannot make ourselves righteous, we need to come to Christ, 'that we might be justified by faith'. Similarly, we want to show our Mormon friends that they too need to come to Christ and be justified by faith.

STEP 1: THE BOOK OF MORMON

First, ask the Mormon missionary to read Moroni 10:32:

> *Yea, come unto Christ, and be perfected in him, and deny yourselves of all ungodliness; and if ye shall deny yourselves of all ungodliness, and love God with all your might, mind and strength, then is his grace sufficient for you, that by his grace ye may be perfect in Christ; and if by the grace of God ye are perfect in Christ, ye can in nowise deny the power of God.*

Next, ask them what this verse means. The main points you want to make are that it says that Latter-day Saints have to deny themselves of all ungodliness and only then is God's grace sufficient. Follow-up questions you could ask are: What would denying yourselves of all ungodliness look like? Would you be perfect? How are you doing in this quest to be completely godly?

Then give them another example of where you need to earn blessing from everyday life. For example, a parent may say to their child, 'If you eat all your broccoli, *then* you can have some ice cream.' Notice how in that scenario the ice cream will only arrive *when* the child does as the parent asked and eats all their broccoli.

That is like another verse in the Book of Mormon: 2 Nephi 25:23, which you should ask them to read:

> *For we labor diligently to write, to persuade our children, and also our brethren, to believe in Christ, and to be reconciled to God; for we know that it is by grace that we are saved, after all we can do.*

Ask your Mormon friend: What does this verse mean? According to it, grace is only available after you have done 'all' you can. Then point out that the meaning here of 'after all we can do' is the equivalent of the meaning of 'then' found in Moroni 10:32. Follow-up questions you could ask are: Have you done all you can do? For example, how long have you prayed or how much of the Book of Mormon have you read today? Whatever their answer, ask: Could you have done more? You are trying to show them that there is always more that they could do and therefore, according to 2 Nephi 25:23, grace will never be given to them.

STEP 2: TRUE TO THE FAITH

True to the Faith is a Latter-day Saints publication that a Mormon will be very familiar with, and may even have a copy with them.

Ask the Mormon missionary to read the following section, which can be found under the heading 'Grace' on page 77:

> The phrase 'after all we can do' teaches that effort is required on our part to receive the fulness of the Lord's grace and be made worthy to dwell with Him. *The Lord has commanded us to obey His gospel,*

> *which includes having faith in Him, repenting of our sins, being baptized, receiving the gift of the Holy Ghost, and enduring to the end (see John 3:3–5; 3 Nephi 27:16–20; Articles of Faith 1:3–4).* The prophet Moroni wrote of the grace we receive as we come unto the Savior and obey His teachings: '*Come unto Christ, and be perfected in him, and deny yourselves of all ungodliness;* and if ye shall deny yourselves of all ungodliness, *and love God with all your might, mind and strength,* then is his grace sufficient for you, *that by his grace ye may be perfect in Christ; and if by the grace of God ye are perfect in Christ, ye can in nowise deny the power of God* (my emphasis).

Then ask them: Have you cleansed yourself of all ungodliness? If they have not, then his grace is *not* sufficient for them.

STEP 3: THE BOOK OF MORMON

This time, ask your Mormon friend to read Alma 11:37:

> *And I say unto you again that he cannot save them in their sins; for I cannot deny his word, and he hath said that no unclean thing can inherit the kingdom of heaven; therefore, how can ye be saved, except ye inherit the kingdom of heaven? Therefore, ye cannot be saved in your sins.*

Once more, ask: What does this verse say? It clearly teaches that to be saved you must deny yourself of all ungodliness and not sin. Follow up by asking: How are you doing at not sinning at all?

As a Mormon cannot be saved in their sins, it is no good them saying, 'I am trying my best' or, 'When I sin, I can just keep on repenting.'

Now ask them to turn to 1 Nephi 3:7 and read it to you:

> *And it came to pass that I, Nephi, said unto my father: I will go and do the things which the Lord hath commanded, for I know that the Lord giveth no commandments unto the children of men, save he shall prepare a way for them that they may accomplish the thing which he commandeth them.*

Follow up by asking: Doesn't this verse say that it is possible to keep the commandments of the Lord? How are you doing at keeping them all?

> **TIP:**
>
> When engaging with a Mormon in this way, make sure you keep them on topic. Don't let them take you elsewhere in conversation and then distract you.

STEP 4: DOCTRINE AND COVENANTS

Doctrine and Covenants is one of the standard Latter-day Saints works.

Ask the Mormon missionary to read Doctrine and Covenants 58:42–43:

> *Behold, he who has repented of his sins, the same is forgiven, and I, the Lord, remember them no more. By this ye may know if a man repenteth of his sins – behold, he will confess them and* forsake them (my emphasis).

TIP:

If a Mormon has not already spoken about how they repent of their sin, they may well do so at this point. For example, they may say, 'I repent every day.' Whilst, of course, we all sin and should therefore confess and repent, point out that according to Mormon doctrine that is not enough. This teaches that the fact they sin every day means they are not truly repenting.

Firstly, put this question to them: What is this doctrine teaching? It is saying that true repentance is not just confessing sins but also forsaking them. Secondly, ask: As, according to this verse, you cannot repent and then commit the same sin again, how are you doing at never sinning again in the same way?

Another example from everyday life may help to reinforce this point. Ask them if, when they get married (or indeed did marry), they will (or did) say that they would forsake all others? Does that mean they will try their best to forsake all others? Or does it mean that if they do sin and cheat on their spouse, they will just consider it acceptable to 'repent' and then start again?

You could also ask your Mormon friend whether they have ever heard this quote from Joseph Smith: 'Repentance is a thing that cannot be trifled with every day. Daily transgression and daily repentance is not that which is pleasing in the sight of God.'[37] Joseph says that God is not happy with daily repentance, even if you think that you're doing your best.

STEP 5: THE MIRACLE OF FORGIVENESS

The Miracle of Forgiveness is a book by the former Mormon prophet Spencer W. Kimball – they will no doubt have a copy of, and may have read, it.

Read the following passage to the Mormon missionary:

> Desire Is Not Sufficient. *In other words, it is not real repentance until one has abandoned the error of his way and started on a new path. Someone has said that there is only one way to quit a bad habit and that is to stop. The saving power does not extend to him*

> *who merely* wants *to change his life. True repentance prods one to action ...* Trying Is Not Sufficient. *Nor is repentance complete when one merely tries to abandon sin ... To try is weak. To do the best you can is not strong. You must always do better than you can. This is true in every walk of life* (my emphasis).[38]

Spencer W. Kimball says here, 'Trying is not sufficient ... To try is weak'. You must actually stop sinning. So follow up this quote by asking: How well are you doing with this need to succeed in stopping all sin? What does this teach you? What sin are you committing that you hope God will overlook? State clearly that, according to what Spencer W. Kimball wrote, God will not overlook your sin.

TIP:

If a Mormon says something along the lines of 'God knows I am doing my best and I believe he will forgive me,' ask them to read Doctrine and Covenants 1:31–33:

CONTINUE ↓

For I the Lord cannot look upon sin with the least degree of allowance; Nevertheless, he that repents and does the commandments of the Lord shall be forgiven; And he that repents not, from him shall be taken even the light which he has received; for my Spirit shall not always strive with man, saith the Lord of Hosts.

This is not the only problem a Mormon has. What if they truly do repent of their sin, but a year or so later recommit the same sin? Ask your Mormon friend if they know what God says about that. Then have them read Doctrine and Covenants 82:7:

> *And now, verily I say unto you, I, the Lord, will not lay any sin to your charge; go your ways and sin no more; but unto that soul who sinneth shall the former sins return, saith the Lord your God.*

Follow up this by asking: What does the Lord say in this verse? He says that if you commit one sin, all your past sins will return!

TIP:

It can be helpful to use the illustration of climbing up a ladder. A Mormon may be doing well and effectively climbing high, but then they will sin. According to Doctrine and Covenants 82:7 above, that means all their past sins will 'return' and knock them to the bottom of the ladder again. How are they ever going to reach the top?

It might be, if the Mormon missionary hasn't already done so, that they say they will have a chance to get things right beyond death in the spirit world. If they do argue that, ask them to read Alma 34:32–35:

> *For behold, this life is the time for men to prepare to meet God; yea, behold the day of this life is the day for men to perform their labors.*
>
> *And now, as I said unto you before, as ye have had so many witnesses, therefore, I beseech of you that ye do not procrastinate the day of your repentance until the end; for after*

> *this day of life, which is given us to prepare for eternity, behold, if we do not improve our time while in this life, then cometh the night of darkness wherein there can be no labor performed.*
>
> *Ye cannot say, when ye are brought to that awful crisis, that I will repent, that I will return to my God. Nay, ye cannot say this; for that same spirit which doth possess your bodies at the time that ye go out of this life, that same spirit will have power to possess your body in that eternal world.*
>
> *For behold, if ye have procrastinated the day of your repentance even until death, behold, ye have become subjected to the spirit of the devil, and he doth seal you his; therefore, the Spirit of the Lord hath withdrawn from you, and hath no place in you, and the devil hath all power over you; and this is the final state of the wicked.*

For one final time, ask: What do these verses teach? Make sure that they understand they must *not* procrastinate and think they can repent in the spirit world. Instead, they need to repent *now*. Follow up by asking: What does this passage say happens to those who don't repent in this life? Its message is very clear: those people get sealed to the devil. That is the final state of the wicked.

By now the Mormons you are speaking to should be aware of their hopeless situation. The gospel they are seeking to follow is impossible. They cannot keep it, nor can it enable them to return to Heavenly Father. These poor lost souls need to hear the good news of the true gospel.

11

JESUS IS ENOUGH

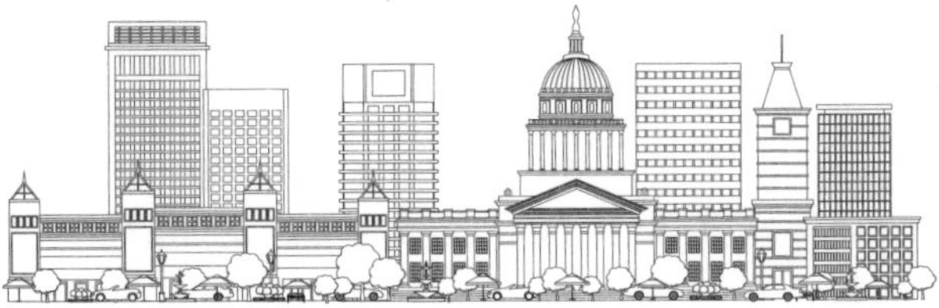

If you manage to dialogue with a Mormon in such a way as suggested in the last chapter, they will find themselves between a rock and a hard place. Now they really have only two options. They can respond by saying either, 'I will just have to work harder' or, 'It's impossible – what can I do?' Of course, we hope and pray for the latter.

'I WILL WORK HARDER'

We need to show our Mormon friends that no amount of work will ever be sufficient to reach Heavenly Father. There are many verses in the Bible that make this clear:

We have all become like one who is unclean, and all our righteous deeds are like a polluted garment. We all fade like a leaf, and our iniquities, like the wind, take us away (Isaiah 64:6).

What then shall we say was gained by Abraham, our forefather according to the flesh? For if Abraham was justified by works, he has something to boast about, but not before God. For what does the Scripture say? 'Abraham believed God, and it was counted to him as righteousness.' Now to the one who works, his wages are not counted as a gift but as his due. And to the one who does not work but believes in him who justifies the ungodly, his faith is counted as righteousness (Romans 4:1–5).

But if it is by grace, it is no longer on the basis of works; otherwise grace would no longer be grace (Romans 11:6).

... we know that a person is not justified by works of the law but through faith in Jesus Christ, so we also have believed in Christ Jesus, in order to be justified by faith in

Christ and not by works of the law, because by works of the law no one will be justified (Galatians 2:16).

I do not nullify the grace of God, for if righteousness were through the law, then Christ died for no purpose (Galatians 2:21).

You are severed from Christ, you who would be justified by the law; you have fallen away from grace (Galatians 5:4).

… he saved us, not because of works done by us in righteousness, but according to his own mercy, by the washing of regeneration and renewal of the Holy Spirit (Titus 3:5).

Like all groups trusting in righteousness by their 'works' or deeds, Mormons need to be shown that they have nothing to offer God. As Jonathan Edwards, the eighteenth-century Puritan, said, 'You contribute nothing to your salvation except the sin that made it necessary.' Having shown the Mormons that we are all sinners in need of grace, we can then begin to point them to the real Jesus.

JESUS HAS DONE ALL THAT IS NEEDED FOR OUR SALVATION

As Mormons begin to realise that the Mormon gospel cannot save them, we have an opportunity to talk about the salvation that is available by grace, through faith in Christ alone.

As we've already mentioned, the gospel of Mormonism is not the gospel of Jesus. The word 'gospel' means 'good news'. Highlight the difference by asking: Do the laws that the Church of Jesus Christ of Latter-day Saints state that you must keep, and that you cannot possibly sustain, sound like good news?

Then explain the good news that they *can* be forgiven of their sins, and that they *can* know for sure that when they die, they will be with Heavenly Father. That is because the good news is that Jesus is enough: he has done all that was necessary to reconcile us back to God. Continue by asking: Can I show you this? Can I explain this to you?

If you get a positive response at this point, praise God for the Holy Spirit is at work. You can then present the gospel by sharing with them God's Word. Below are some passages that can be used, depending on how the Holy Spirit leads you. The good news we want to keep emphasising is that, though we do not deserve forgiveness, we receive it by faith in Jesus.

> ... *for all have sinned and fall short of the glory of God,* and are justified by his grace as a gift, through the redemption that is in Christ Jesus, *whom God put forward as a propitiation by his blood, to be received by faith. This was to show God's righteousness, because in his divine forbearance he had passed over former sins. It was to show his righteousness at the present time, so that he might be just and the justifier of the one who has faith in Jesus (Romans 3:23–26,* my emphasis).

God acquits people and declares them to be innocent of their sin because Jesus paid for our debt on the cross. Jesus therefore fulfilled the law for us:

> *Do not think that I have come to abolish the Law or the Prophets; I have not come to abolish them but to fulfil them (Matthew 5:17).*

> *For God has done what the law, weakened by the flesh, could not do. By sending his own Son in the likeness of sinful flesh and for sin, he condemned sin in the flesh, in order that the righteous requirement of the law might be fulfilled in us, who walk not according to the flesh but according to the Spirit (Romans 8:3–4).*

> *For Christ is the end of the law for righteousness to everyone who believes (Romans 10:4).*

In fulfilling the law on our behalf, Jesus can forgive us of our sins:

> *The saying is trustworthy and deserving of full acceptance, that Christ Jesus came into the world to save sinners (1 Timothy 1:15).*

> *And there is salvation in no one else, for there is no other name under heaven given among men by which we must be saved (Acts 4:12).*

> *[The Philippian jailer] said, 'Sirs, what must I do to be saved?' And they [Paul and Silas] said, 'Believe in the Lord Jesus, and*

> *you will be saved, you and your household' (Acts 16:30–31).*

> *All this is from God, who through Christ reconciled us to himself and gave us the ministry of reconciliation; that is, in Christ God was reconciling the world to himself, not counting their trespasses against them, and entrusting to us the message of reconciliation (2 Corinthians 5:18–19).*

> *For our sake he made him to be sin who knew no sin, so that in him we might become the righteousness of God (2 Corinthians 5:21).*

We trust that, as we use the Word of God, the Holy Spirit will do his work and bring Mormons to the point of realising that Jesus is enough. At this point we long to hear the words 'What must I do to be saved?' We can then lead them in prayer for their salvation.

12

SHARING THE GOSPEL WITH MORMONS

I am astonished that you are so quickly deserting him who called you in the grace of Christ and are turning to a different gospel – not that there is another one, but there are some who trouble you and want to distort the gospel of Christ. But even if we or an angel from heaven should preach to you a gospel contrary to the one we preached to you, let him be accursed. As we have said before, so now I say again: If anyone is preaching to you a gospel contrary to the one you received, let him be accursed (Galatians 1:6–9).

We have established beyond any doubt that Mormonism and biblical Christianity are vastly different. The Apostle Paul's words to the Galatians, above, could have been written to the Mormon Church. Joseph Smith claimed to have been visited by an angel from heaven who gave him a gospel contrary to the one Paul preached. The Church of Jesus Christ of Latter-day Saints have deserted the grace of Christ and have turned to a different gospel. Consequently, they are lost and in need of a Saviour.

If you have tried to share the gospel with Mormons, I am sure you, like me, have found it a hugely frustrating experience. Though they are often pleasant to speak to and don't run away immediately when challenged, their testimony of the truth that they believe can seem impenetrable. Please let me remind you of that which you already know – we cannot save anyone!

People are not won for Christ by clever argumentation or a slick methodology; they are won by the Holy Spirit, often working through a believer who shares the gospel truth in love. Therefore, there is no silver bullet to how to bring someone to a saving faith in Christ, only tips, advice, observations and prayer.

KNOW WHAT YOU BELIEVE AND WHY

In speaking with Mormons, it is important to know not only the key tenets of the Christian faith but also why you believe them. Mormons believe things because they 'feel' they are true, or they have had an experience (a 'burning in the bosom') that they think confirms that something is true. In contrast, Christianity is not a blind faith but a reasoned one. Whilst we do have feelings and experiences, all such things are to be tested against the Word of God – the Bible. The Bereans were commended for doing exactly this in Acts 17:11:

> *Now these Jews were more noble than those in Thessalonica; they received the word with all eagerness, examining the Scriptures daily to see if these things were so.*

We too are instructed to give a defence of what we believe:

> *Have no fear of them, nor be troubled, but in your hearts honour Christ the Lord as holy, always being prepared to make a defence to anyone who asks you for a reason for the hope that is in you; yet do it with gentleness and respect, having a good conscience, so that, when you are slandered, those who revile your good behaviour in Christ may be put to shame (1 Peter 3:14–16).*

We are to give a defence 'with gentleness and respect'.

TRY NOT TO SEEM CONTENTIOUS

Being gentle and respectful is especially important when dealing with Mormons, because of what they have been taught:

> *'He that hath the spirit of contention is not of me,' said the Lord, 'but is of the devil, who is the father of contention, and he stirreth up the hearts of men to contend with anger, one with another (3 Nephi 11:29).*

Mormons do not like 'contention'. If they believe you are becoming argumentative, overexcited or aggressive in your tone, they may say you have 'the spirit of contention' – the 'c' word. This is not a good thing. They are claiming you are being devilish. Furthermore, if they believe you are being contentious, they may decide the conversation is over and leave. Therefore, it is important that we exhibit the fruit of the Spirit in our dialogue with them.

TIP:

On occasion I have had Mormons become a little overexcited and aggressive in their responses towards me. If this happens to you, suggest they are being contentious and you will find they quickly calm down and even apologise. After all, they do not want to be seen to be in allegiance with the 'father of contention'.

AVOID BEING LABELLED 'ANTI-MORMON'

Also be aware that if we become contentious, we will be labelled anti-Mormon. This charge usually comes if we speak against Joseph Smith or any of their prophets, or if we use another 'c' word – 'cult'! Whilst there will be times when we need to speak to them about their prophets, we need to be careful. Speaking ill of Joseph Smith is the equivalent of disparaging the Pope to a Catholic, or Moses to a Jew. As for using the word 'cult', I find it best to call them a new religious movement. This is less offensive to them and doesn't cause them to bring the anti-Mormon charge.

ASK QUESTIONS TO UNDERSTAND MORMONISM

It is good to know something about what Mormons believe – though this is less important than knowing what we believe. So ask questions to clarify what Mormonism teaches. Even if you think you have some understanding of the Mormon gospel, rather than saying, 'You believe … don't you?' it is better to ask, 'Can you please tell me what you believe about …?' This is important because, unlike the Jehovah's Witnesses, individual Mormons can greatly vary on what they both understand and believe.

TIP:

If you asked ten Jehovah's Witnesses the same question, you will receive ten identical answers. If you ask ten Mormons the same question, you will receive fifteen different answers! Why is this? There are a couple of reasons. Firstly, Mormonism has so many competing and contradictory scriptures and authorities that individual Mormons can pick and choose from them. This means that individual Mormons can often find themselves at odds with official Mormon doctrine. Secondly, not all Mormons experience the same things. For example, the majority of Mormons have never been in the temple, so are not aware of the things taught and practised there.

FOCUS ON GOD'S GRACE

Mormons are greatly burdened by all the laws and ordinances that they have been told to keep. They speak of grace but know nothing of it. How they need to be washed and set free by the grace of the Lord Jesus. The following verses are very good to share with our Mormon friends:

And by that will we have been sanctified through the offering of the body of Jesus Christ once for all.

And every priest stands daily at his service, offering repeatedly the same sacrifices, which can never take away sins. But when Christ had offered for all time a single sacrifice for sins, he sat down at the right hand of God, waiting from that time until his enemies should be made a footstool for his feet. For by a single offering he has perfected for all time those who are being sanctified.

And the Holy Spirit also bears witness to us; for after saying,

'This is the covenant that I will make with them
after those days, declares the Lord:
I will put my laws on their hearts,
and write them on their minds,'

then he adds,

'I will remember their sins and their lawless deeds no more.'

> *Where there is forgiveness of these, there is no longer any offering for sin (Hebrews 10:10–18,* my emphasis*).*

Mormons believe that they must be perfect because, after all, didn't Jesus say, 'Be ye therefore perfect, even as your Father which is in heaven is perfect' (Matthew 5:48, KJV)? All their striving is towards this end of perfection, but they can never attain it. None of us can. That is why we need Jesus. The writer to the Hebrews tells us above that Jesus, by his offering, has perfected for ever them that are sanctified. This is a powerful verse for all Mormons to hear. It blows apart their belief in righteousness by their works and shows them that Jesus has done all that is necessary for them to be forgiven.

These verses say even more than that. We are sanctified (that is, made holy) through Jesus' offering of himself on the cross. Priests can never take away sins. However, the Holy Spirit witnesses to both these facts and adds the powerful truth that God will remember no more our sins and iniquities. Jesus is enough.

> *He [Jesus] himself bore our sins in his body on the tree, that we might die to sin and live to righteousness. By his wounds you have been healed (1 Peter 2:24).*

> *For by grace you have been saved through faith. And this is not your own doing; it is the gift of God, not a result of works, so that no one may boast (Ephesians 2:8–9).*

These verses, coupled with others, can be used to show that there is no work we can do to appear righteous in God's sight. We can never be perfect, and so we must rest in the finished work of Jesus. Grace is what Mormons need.

PRAY FOR AND LOVE MORMONS

I began this book by saying that I love Mormons but I do not love Mormonism. Friends, if we are to reach them with the gospel of grace, we need to have this insight ever before us. We need to separate individual Mormons from what binds them, and instead see them as lost people for whom Jesus died. Jesus came into the world to seek and save that which is lost. Let's seek to share the good news with them and pray for them.

> *Brothers, my heart's desire and prayer to God for them is that they may be saved. For I bear them witness that they have a zeal for God, but not according to knowledge. For, being ignorant of the righteousness of God, and seeking to establish their own, they did not submit to God's righteousness. For Christ is the end of the law for righteousness to everyone who believes (Romans 10:1–4).*

If we were to take the word 'them' from the first sentence above and replace it with 'Mormons', the passage would still make sense. Mormons are zealous for God, but their zeal is misplaced. They do not know the righteousness of God found in Jesus, so they seek to establish their own. Like Paul, may our heart's desire and prayer to God for Mormons be that they may be saved.

RECOMMENDED RESOURCES

Mormon – Biblical Investigation Series by Michael Thomas (available to buy through Reachout Trust: https://reachouttrust.org/?s=mormon+investigation+series)

Mormonism, a Gold-Plated Religion by Mike and Ann Thomas (available to buy through Reachout Trust: https://reachouttrust.org/product/mormonism-gold-plated-religion-mike-ann-thomas/)

Unveiling Grace: The Story of How We Found Our Way Out of the Mormon Church by Lynn K. Wilder (Zondervan, 2013).

Passport to Heaven: The True Story of a Zealous Mormon Missionary Who Discovers the Jesus He Never Knew by Micah Wilder (Harvest House Publishers, 2021 – and available to buy through 10ofthose.com).

For more information on Mormonism, also contact Reachout Trust: www.reachouttrust.org

REACHOUT TRUST
BUILDING A BRIDGE OF REASON

Reachout offers a ministry of Christian apologetics, counter-cult apologetics, relevant news stories and encouragement to Christian believers in order *'to contend for the faith that was once for all entrusted to the saints'* (Jude 3, NRSV). We aim to do this by means of a regular e-newsletter, books, tracts, our website, recordings, seminars, sermons and workshops.

NOTES

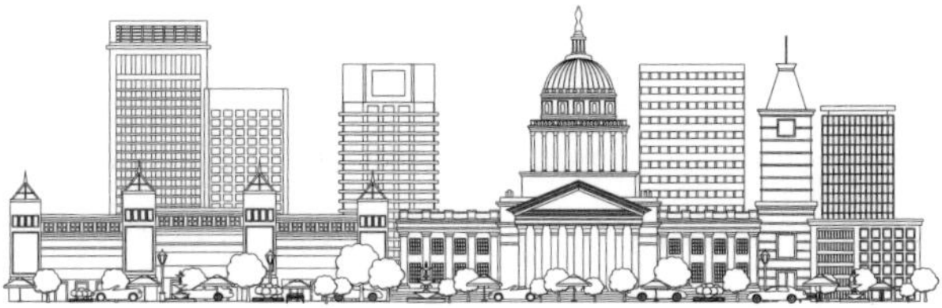

1 Joseph Fielding Smith, Mormon prophet and former President (and the nephew of the Mormon founder Joseph Smith), Stake Conference Message, 2 November 1891 – taken from *Collected Discourses* 2:305.

2 Thomas S. Monson, Mormon prophet and former President, speaking at the church's general conference, October 2012.

3 John Piper, *Finally Alive: What Happens When We Are Born Again?* (Christian Focus Publications, 2009), pp. 165–166.

4 Gordon B. Hinckley, Mormon prophet and former President: http://www.bbc.co.uk/religion/religions/mormon/beliefs/christian.shtml

5 Harold B. Lee was a Mormon prophet and former President. Taken from Clyde J. Williams (ed.), *The Teachings of Harold B. Lee* (1996), p. 371, quoted in 'Joseph Smith, Restorer of Truth', *Ensign*, December 2003.

6 Joseph Fielding Smith, *Doctrines of Salvation* 1:188.

7 Gordon B. Hinckley, 'The Marvellous Foundation of our Faith,' *Ensign* (Conference Edition), November 2002, p. 80.

8 See (https://www.churchofjesuschrist.org/study/manual/gospel-topics/first-vision?lang=eng). Where Joseph Smith's own words are quoted, these are taken from his *History of the Church* – see vol. 1, pp. 16–17 and 19. See also *Teachings of Presidents of the Church: Joseph Smith* (2007), p. 438; and *Times and Seasons*, 1 March 1842, p. 707.

9 Joseph Smith, *History of the Church*, vol. 1, pp. 5–6.

10 Thomas S. Monson, speaking at the church's conference in Salt Lake City, 2005.

11 'Praise to the Man': William W. Phelps, 1792–1872.

12 Brigham Young, Mormon prophet and former President, 9 October 1859 – taken from *Journal of Discourses* 7:28.

13 Joseph Smith, *History of the Church*, vol. 4, p. 461.

14 The character Elder Cunningham in the musical *The Book of Mormon* by Trey Parker, Robert Lopez and Matt Stone (2011).

15 Ezra Taft Benson, Mormon prophet and former President, *A Witness and a Warning* (1988), p. vii.

16 *The Teachings of Ezra Taft Benson* (1988), p. 557.

17 Joseph Smith, *History of the Church*, vol. 1, pp. 33–34.

18 https://www.churchofjesuschrist.org/study/new-era/2020/04/q-a/how-did-joseph-smith-translate-the-book-of-mormon?lang=eng

19 Joseph Fielding Smith, *Conference Reports*, April 1880, p. 36.

20 Joseph Fielding Smith, *Doctrines of Salvation* 2:16.

21 Rulon S. Wells, *Conference Reports*, April 1937, p. 72.

22 Spencer W. Kimball was a Mormon prophet and former President. Taken from *Teachings of the Presidents of the Church: Spencer W. Kimball* (1962), p. 8.

23 Joseph Fielding Smith, *Doctrines of Salvation* 2:219.

24 Joseph Smith, King Follett sermon at a church conference in Nauvoo, Illinois, 7 April 1844.

25 *Church News* of the Church of Jesus Christ of Latter-day Saints, 20 June 1998, p. 7.

26 This suggestion was first made by Walter Martin: 'When people say, "I believe in Jesus", look them straight in the eye and ask, "Which one?"'

27 James Talmage, Mormon Apostle, *The Articles of Faith*, pp. 466–467.

28 Joseph Fielding Smith, *Gospel Doctrine* (1986), p. 68.

29 *The Teachings of Spencer W. Kimball* (1962), pp. 32–33.

30 Bruce R. McConkie, Mormon Apostle, *Mormon Doctrine* (1966), p. 323.

31 Milton R. Hunter, Mormon Council member, *The Gospel through the Ages* (1945), p. 51.

32 Gordon B. Hinckley, 'We look to Christ', *Ensign* (Conference Edition), May 2002, p. 90.

33 *Preach My Gospel*, p. 61.

34 *Teachings of the Prophet Joseph Smith* (1938), p. 370.

35 James R. White, *The Forgotten Trinity* (Bethany House, 1998), p. 26.

36 Keith Walker *(Evidence Ministries)* took elements of the teachings of Bill McKeever (Mormon Research Institute), Timothy Oliver *(Think About Eternity)*, and Tim Martin (The Center for Apologetics Research: CFAR) and developed what Keith named: *The Impossible Gospel.*

37 Joseph Smith, *History of the Church*, vol. 3, pp. 379–381.

38 Spencer W. Kimball, *The Miracle of Forgiveness* (1969), pp. 164–165.

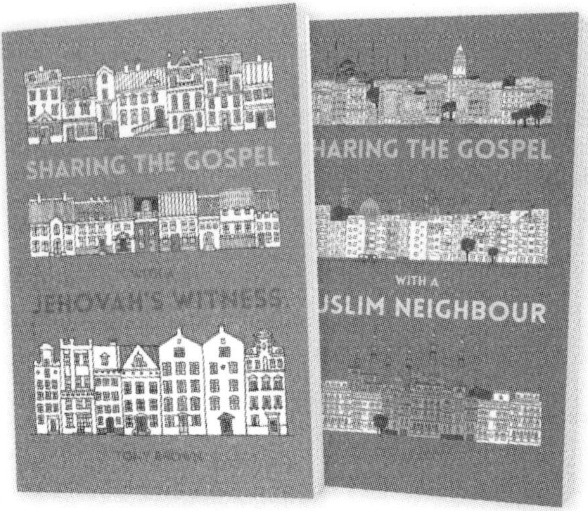

10 Publishing

10Publishing is committed to publishing quality Christian resources that are biblical, accessible and point people to Jesus.

www.10ofthose.com is our online retail partner selling thousands of quality books at discounted prices.

For information contact: **info@10ofthose.com**
or check out our website: **www.10ofthose.com**